PRAISE FOR *TEN BIG WORDS*

"God was the original tweeter. He understood powerful messages could be sent in short form and would be remembered. Literally any time you take a moment to focus on these truths you are shaping your mind, life, character and future. I am so glad Abby took the initiative to gather God's word in the form of *Ten Big Words*. Students, children, adults, anyone who touches the content will be marked. Enjoy the journey."

~Beth Guckenberger, author of *Reckless Faith*,
Relentless Hope and the *Tales Series*
Executive Director of Back2Back Ministries

"Having been a youth pastor for 15 years, I am always looking for great material to use with students. Abby has done a fantastic job making memorizing scripture simple and applicable. I am very excited to incorporate *Ten Big Words* into our small group teachings and watching our kids hide the Word of God in their hearts."

~Amy Reger, Director of Student Ministry
Horizon Community Church

"Memorizing scripture is such a powerful tool to stay Christ centered, to remember how much He loves us, that He is always there for us, that He will give us the strength we need. But sometimes memorization can be daunting. Where should you start? *Ten Big Words* is a fantastic tool to help kids, teens and their parents memorize some key Bible verses. It's simple, straightforward and fun. *Ten Big Words* gives great strategies and insights for keeping God's word where we can always reach it, written on our hearts."

~Laura L. Smith, author of
It's Complicated, It's Over and *It's Addicting*

"I wish I had this book when my oldest two were entering their teen years. The teenage years are wrought with lies that society tells them about who they are and what they should be. *Ten Big Words* gives tweens and teens the ability to memorize God's truths about who they really are and who they are meant to be."

~Sarah Youngblood, Youth Minister

"*Ten Big Words* made learning Bible verses simple, by tearing them out and hanging them on my mirror. Throughout the week I saw connections from the verses to my life. I would recommend this book to other teens for weekly inspiration."

~Kennedy M. (age 14)

TEN BIG WORDS

10-Word Bible Verses for Teens

ABBY BOLDT MESSNER

Ten Big Words
10-Word Bible Verses for Teens

for j, s & a

...my loves

Contents

INTRODUCTION

I was helping out with the fifth and sixth graders at church last year when the kids were charged with memorizing Bible verses. All the other adults seemed to think this was a fantastic idea, but inwardly I was cringing.

I remembered having to memorize a poem in elementary school and how stressful it was for me. It gave me hives. Not real hives, just the mental ones...but trust me, they're just as troublesome.

There were a few kids who appeared to be in their element memorizing poems. They actually seemed to be *enjoying* it, if that's even possible. But I could tell that there were others like me: the distraught ones. And there were distraught ones in the room whose eyes got very big at the mention of memorizing Bible verses.

But God has great timing. Shortly after I spotted those big eyes, I heard Lysa TerKeurst being interviewed on the radio about a ten-word Bible verse she taught her daughter to memorize by counting the words on their fingers. When her daughter was in a stressful situation, she recalled the verse, and it brought her comfort and confidence.

So not only had her daughter memorized it, she had applied it in her life!

This was the answer for the distraught ones! I was so excited I immediately started googling ten-word verses, fully assuming someone else had already figured this out.

They hadn't!

I couldn't find anything to share with my wide-eyed friends at church, so I decided to take matters into my own hands and do it myself. Necessity is the mother of all invention, right?

I began collecting verses that day from the Internet, a Bible app, my Bible, and anything else I could find that had Bible verses in it. These verses come from all different translations of the Bible, so just consider it a melting pot of God's goodness blended together to shine on our kids.

So there you have it: humble beginnings and an unlikely person—me—called to fill a need.

And why am I unlikely, you ask?

The short answer is this:

I arrived late in the game to this Jesus thing.

The long answer:

Well, I grew up going to church every week but never felt connected to God. Ever. It was formal, and none of it seemed very accessible to me.

Fast-forward to a few years after my kids were born and my husband, Jay, and I decided it was probably time for our family to go to church. It seemed like the 'right' way to raise kids and the responsible thing to do. I fully expected a repeat performance of my youth: an obligation fulfilled on Sundays that gave no return on the investment of time.

Boy was I wrong. Thanks to the recommendation of a few friends and the sheer luck of its proximity, we found a church that spoke to us—that swiped God off His golden seat on high and plunked Him right next to us in our lives. In our messy, ordinary lives.

I would be lying if I didn't say my relationship with God was a little awkward at first. I sort of forgot that He already knows everything, so I tried to make a good impression by being the right version of me instead of the real one. That was exhausting. Since then, I have been slowly opening up to Him and allowing Him access to me for the first time in my life. Not to the "formal church" me, just plain old me.

So I was on this journey with Him but was starting to feel like I'd never get "there" in my relationship with God. I didn't really know where "there" was, but I envisioned a higher spirituality or certain holiness would overtake me. Thank goodness a friend reminded me that you never really get "there." There's no if/then equation that makes me worthy or deserving of God's love and grace. Everyone's journey with Him is different, and that's okay. It's making yourself available to Him that's the key.

The first time I counted out a Bible verse on my fingers and then used it in a real life situation, I knew I was onto something and felt compelled to share it. My experience was empowering and confidence building, and when I said the words, it was like inviting God into a part of my day that I normally would have experienced alone.

I knew that if I could arm kids with this incredible and simple tool, they would grow spiritually and be just a little more equipped to deal with life.

I would never in a million years have predicted that I could compile a book of Bible verses. But the Lord works in mysterious ways, and this is what my being available to Him looks like.

So there you have it.

Now let's get counting!

GETTING STARTED

There are enough verses in *Ten Big Words* to learn one per week for a year (with a two-week vacation built in, because let's face it, you're busy!). Each Bible verse is 10 words long, and as you read it, count the words out on your fingers or toes or whatever you have available. Using this method makes it super easy to remember!

Every verse is followed by a few sentences to help you connect with it and apply it in your life, and finally, a question to get you thinking. Just memorizing the verse is great. Using it to help you through a tough time or in celebration is even better!

Ten Big Words was created to make memorizing Bible verses easy and relevant to you as a teenager. Don't worry if your favorite translation of the Bible doesn't match *Ten Big Word's* verse exactly. Remember, the idea is to make it simple to get into the Bible through memorization. To do this, different translations were used to fit within the 10-word structure. And in a few cases, *Ten Big Words* has taken a powerful 10-word phrase from a longer verse because it had such great impact.

HERE ARE A FEW WAYS TO GET STARTED:

- Find a friend. Having a partner will make it easier to stay on track.
- Post the verse on your favorite social media site and get a big group to join you.
- Get out your Bible and use sticky notes to flag the verses you learn. At the end of the year, you will be amazed at how much of the Bible you have experienced.
- Make it a family affair. Pull your book out and have it be the topic of conversation one night a week at dinner.
- Download a Bible app to keep the verses handy. YouVersion is a good one.

This book was designed for you to use it, so don't be afraid to make notes in it or fold down the pages of the verses that really speak to you. Go ahead, rip out a verse and post it in your locker or give one to a friend.

Challenge yourself to learn one new verse a week.

You've got this!

Just be faithful and available.
God will piece the rest of the story together.

~Beth Guckenberger
Back2Back Ministries

CHAPTER 1
GOD'S WOW FACTOR

OUR GOD IS AMAZING. He is a miracle maker and creator of all. Stop what you're doing right now and look in a mirror or look outside. He did that. As you read and learn the verses in this chapter, spend some time thinking about how He is great in your life and in your world.

In the beginning God created the
Heavens and the earth.

Genesis 1.1

It all started here...Sometimes we forget how all-powerful our God is. He created EVERYTHING. All of it. He was masterful in making us and the world we live in.

Doesn't it make sense to put our trust in our maker?

God said, "Let there be light,"
and there was light.

Genesis 1.3

These are the first words spoken in the Bible; God said this when He created the heavens and the earth. When you wrap yourself in God's light, others take note of your glow.

Will you make it your mission to shine?

I praise You because I am
fearfully and wonderfully made.

Psalm 139.14

Spend a few minutes thinking about how the human body
works. Amazing, right? God created you, and you are mirac-
ulous with every breath you take.

What are ways you can honor your body?

Our Father which art in Heaven,
hallowed be thy name.

Matthew 6.9

This is the prayer Jesus taught His disciples when they asked Him how to pray. Hallowed means respected and revered, but don't worry, your prayers don't have to be formal…He just loves to hear from you!

What would you say to Him right now?

Things that are impossible with
men are possible with God.

Luke 18.27

Ever hear of a little thing called a miracle? Those come from
the Man upstairs. With Him by your side, anything is possible. Anything.

**Can you talk to God about what seems
impossible in your life right now?**

*We have different gifts, according
to the grace given us.*

Romans 12.6

He made you to be you, an individual...so be the *Great YOU* that He intended. Don't compare yourself to others. Just be the best you that you can be.

How do you use your gifts?

For the earth is the Lord's and everything in it.

Psalm 24

Remember, it's His earth, and we are here to take care of it. Marvel at everything your eyes see.

How can you be a good steward of the spaces you keep?

Be strong in the Lord and in
His mighty power.

Ephesians 6.10

Life can get hard. If you use Him as your shield, God will
take you where you were meant to be.

Have you talked to Him about the path you're on?

CHAPTER 2
GOD IS GOOD

good (adj):
virtuous, right, commendable, kind, benevolent
Merriam-Webster.com

Our God is all things good. He knows we aren't perfect though, so He gave us Jesus — the perfect example of how to act, treat others, and love unconditionally.

He heals the broken hearted and
binds up their wounds.

Psalm 147.3

God gives us the capacity to heal when we have suffered a loss. Healing enables us to take the hurt and learn something about ourselves. These are the times God wants you to sink into Him for comfort.

How do you need His comfort now?

God resists the proud, but gives
grace to the humble.

Proverbs 3.34

Don't act like you are better than anyone else. We are all loved equally in God's eyes. Besides, you'll miss out on all the little gifts God puts in your path if your nose is in the air.

What are ways you can try to stay humble?

He gives strength to the weary and
strengthens the powerless.

Isaiah 40.29

God can help you handle your tough times in ways you
would not be able to by yourself. It's amazing what you are
capable of when you invite God along for the ride.

What makes you feel weary or powerless right now?

Those who hope in the Lord
will renew their strength.

Isaiah 40.31

There will likely be some scary situations in your life, where you feel helpless, and the only thing you can control is your ability to hope. Remember, God never leaves your side. Draw strength from His presence.

In what ways have you experienced His presence?

For my yoke is easy and my burden is light.

Matthew 11.30

A yoke? It's an old-fashioned word for harness...like on a pair of horses or oxen used to pull something heavy. When God is in your life, even the hard times seem better because He is with you. If you let Him, He will help carry some of the weight of your world so you don't have to.

Will you let Him help you?

If God is for us, who can be against us?

Romans 8.31

When you realize God has your back, you can move mountains!

What is the mountain in your life right now?

You are all sons of God through faith in Jesus.

Galatians 3.26

Enjoy this awesome family, and remember that you are connected to every single person through God. It's one giant family, and you are a special part of it.

Will you think of everyone differently
knowing they are family?

Grace be with those who love
our Lord in sincerity.

Ephesians 6.24

Did you earn God's forgiveness? Nope. But it's yours. Without question or judgment.

Has your ability to forgive surprised anyone?

CHAPTER 3
GOD = ♥

It all comes down to LOVE. If we gave more of it away, the world would be a better place!

God = ♥

Hatred stirs up conflict, but love
covers over all wrongs.

Proverbs 10.12

Give love. That's *always* the right answer. God wants you
to put your efforts toward goodness and deal with conflict
openly. No hidden agenda for you.

**Have you ever stirred up conflict? What
do you think about it now?**

God = ♥

Love your enemies and pray for
those who persecute you.

Matthew 5.44

This is a tough one…but remember that God forgives everyone their sins. All of them. Think about His generosity and
try not to be stingy with yours.

Did this bring someone to mind?
What can you do about it?

God = ♥

Love does not delight in evil,
but rejoices in truth.

1 Corinthians 13.6

Love is the answer. God's example is unconditional love to us. The best thing we can do is live our days giving our love to others.

Can you think of someone who needs some love?

God = ❤

Faith, hope, love; and the
greatest of these is love.

1 Corinthians 13.13

Love is the trump card that Jesus gave us to play as often as
we want to in the game of life. It's always a winner, and we
have an unlimited, lifetime supply to give away. Like money,
you can't take it with you, so start giving it away today!

How will you give yours away?

Follow the way of love and
eagerly desire spiritual gifts.

1 Corinthians 14.1

God asks each of us to follow in His footsteps as best we can. His dream is for us to learn about His teachings and marvel at how they fill us up.

What is your favorite Bible story?

God = ♥

God is not the author of
confusion, but of peace.

1 Corinthians 14.33

When you lean on God, things get less complicated because
He speaks one language...that of love. Life is simpler when
we make it our mission to just give love.

Who do you give love to?

Every good gift and every
perfect gift is from above.

James 1.17

Gifts of love and grace are always perfect and good! Accept and enjoy these gifts, then package them up and give them away. God will be pleased.

Who might need these gifts from you?

Finally, all of you, live in
harmony with one another.

1 Peter 3.8

God just wants us to accept and hopefully appreciate one
another for who we are.

Who do you need to live in better harmony with?

CHAPTER 4
CHARACTER

WHO YOU ARE
...WHO *ARE* YOU, ANYWAY?

What are the qualities that are unique to your character? Learning about and following the teachings of the Bible will lift your character to new heights!

The Lord detests lying lips, but
delights in the truth.

Proverbs 12.22

The truth is freeing but sometimes can be hard to speak. Lies will weigh you down and hang heavy in your life, standing between you and God. Make it your mission to let nothing come between you and your God.

Have you ever told the truth in a tough situation?

Where your treasure is, there
your heart will be also.

Matthew 6.21

What you think about becomes what is important. This is worth repeating: What you think about becomes what is important. Try turning your thoughts toward Jesus and see what happens.

**What do you think about? Do you place
importance on what others think?**

In the way you love others,
you will be judged.

Matthew 7.2

Yikes. It's a hard thing not to judge a book by its cover, isn't it? God loves us all just the same, rich or poor, clean or dirty, big or small. Remember that there's always at least one thing in someone's life you know nothing about.

**When has someone surprised you by not
being what you originally thought?**

Love your enemies, do good
to those who hate you.

Luke 6.27

If Jesus hadn't already shown us how to do this, it would seem almost impossible, right? His example is proof that it can be done.

Is there someone who thinks you are an enemy that you could surprise with your goodness?

Be joyful in hope, patient in
affliction, faithful in prayer.

Romans 12.12

The happy stuff, the scary stuff and all the stuff in between
makes you who you are. Try to embrace every bit of it…
the good, bad and ugly, because Jesus has a plan. Consistent
communication with Him will make the highs even better
and the lows bearable.

Have you checked in with Him lately?

Set your mind on things above,
not on earthly things.

Colossians 3.2

Stuff and things won't fill you up in a meaningful way. That sort of emptiness, though, can be remedied by having a relationship with Jesus.

Have you ever thought a certain THING would change your life? How long did it take you to find out it didn't?

Don't share in the sins of others.
Keep yourself pure.

1 Timothy 5.22

Peer pressure stinks. It can knock you off the right path in the blink of an eye. But it can also be hard to stand strong in your beliefs. Just know that following the crowd will empty your tanks, while following Jesus will fill them up.

How have you experienced peer pressure?

Man is justified by works,
and not by faith only.

James 2.24

God loves to see you in action. Don't hold back. Give of yourself; you will never be emptied but overflowing with love.

Have you ever been a volunteer?
How did it make you feel?

The tongue is a little member
and boasts great things.

James 3.5

Watch what you say; your words have power. You can cast shadows or shine light—the choice is yours.

***How have you cast shadows? How
have you shined your light?***

CHAPTER 5
LEAN ON ME

When you have a relationship with God, you will feel Him near you. Take comfort in that when times get tough. When things are going well, take comfort that He had something to do with it. Has there been a time when you've felt Him near you and it brought peace?

The Lord is my lamp; He
turns darkness to light.

2 Samuel 22.29

With God in your heart, even the darkest of days are doable.
Through God, you have the power to turn things around.

What kind of darkness have you struggled with?

The Lord is good, a refuge in times of trouble.

Nahum 1.7

Lean into God. He can handle anything you throw His way. You can always escape into Jesus' love; it will be a refuge for you when things get hard.

Need to get away? Just say Jesus.

Blessed are the meek, for they
shall inherit the earth.

Matthew 5.5

When Jesus said these words to His followers, He wanted them to know, like He wants you to know now, that good guys don't finish last. However, in this life you will have to endure hard things — but those who have faith in Him will ultimately find their reward in heaven.

Has there been a time when you have felt powerless? How did you handle it?

Since we have such a hope, we are very bold.

2 Corinthians 3.12

God gives us confidence to be who we were meant to be. He helps us live fully — unafraid.

***Do you have confidence to be yourself,
or do you follow the crowd?***

Where the spirit of the Lord
is there is freedom.

2 Corinthians 3.17

This freedom helps you not get caught up in unimportant dramas that drag you down. His freedom lifts you up.

***Do you need to be lifted out of a
drama? Ask Him for help.***

I can do all things through Christ
who strengthens me.

Philippians 4.13

Don't give up! You can do it; you can get through it —
because God is with you.

How has God strengthened you?
Who did you tell about it?

Never will I leave you; never
will I forsake you.

Hebrews 13.5

Never. No matter what. There's nothing you can do to scare
Him away. He will forever be by your side, and you can take
comfort in that.

**What are some other things in your life that
will never change that you take comfort in?**

The Lord is my helper; I will not be afraid.

Hebrews 13.6

God is leading your way. Trust His path for you and take comfort that He is with you on the happy days as well as the scary ones.

***Can you think of a few situations
when you have been afraid?***

CHAPTER 6
IN GOD WE TRUST

How do you get to a place where you trust something you cannot see? That's a very good question. For some, it's reading stories about Jesus or talking with trusted friends who trust in God. For others, prayer forms a bond that leads to trust. Everyone gets there differently, and that's okay. What do you think will lead you there?

He is a shield to all who trust in Him.

Psalm 18.30

Let God deflect negativity for you. By trusting in Him, His plan for your life will be possible.

***Has your trust in God shielded you
from something? What?***

Rest in the Lord; wait patiently for Him to act.

Psalm 37.7

Have you ever felt impatient? God's timing isn't necessarily OUR timing. Trust that *He* knows what is best for your life. Watching the clock tick is hard, but often times we learn valuable things while we wait.

Have you learned a lesson waiting on God's timing?

I waited patiently for the
Lord; He heard my cry.

Psalm 40.1

Let's face it, waiting is no fun. Frequently God's agenda is different than ours, which requires a patience we must dig deep to find. Keep in mind that His timing is perfect even though it might not always feel that way.

When was a time you had to wait?

When I'm in trouble I will call out to you.

Psalm 86.7

No matter what you've done, call to God. He will answer you. He wants to walk through life with you, especially when it's an uphill climb, and even if you don't feel that you deserve it. Hint: He thinks you do.

Has there been a time when you have felt unworthy? How did you get past it?

Your Father knows what you
need before you ask him.

Matthew 6.8

God already knows what you are thinking, but He still loves
to hear from you. Reach out to Him and share!

**Is there something you have been avoiding? God's
been waiting for you to come to Him about it.**

Do not let your heart be
troubled. Trust in God.

John 14.1

Are you a worrier? God wants you to hand over that worry
to Him and trust that things will work out the way they
are supposed to. In both good times and bad, place your
confidence in God.

Can you think of one thing you can turn over to God?

God will supply all your needs
according to His riches.

Philippians 4.19

God provides what we need, not necessarily what we want. And what *are* His riches anyway? His word. And living according to His word will fulfill you more than things or money ever could.

**Have you ever wanted something you
didn't get, only to realize later that not
getting it was the best thing for you?**

Cast all your anxiety on Him.
He cares for you.

1 Peter 5.7

Give your problems to God. Talk to Him about what troubles you have and lean into Him for support. He wants so badly to be in a relationship with you.

***Is there anything holding you back from
pursuing a relationship with Jesus?***

The Lord knows how to rescue
Godly men from trials.

2 Peter 2.9

Having God in your life is like having a built-in search and rescue team. Knowing He has your back gives you a feeling of security.

Have you ever felt stranded?

Congratulations, you did it! Way to go! You are now the proud owner of fifty memorized Bible verses. Hopefully you were able to memorize *and* connect with the verses, because that's how they will really come in handy. Pulling one out during a tough time can help ease your burden, or it can take your happy to a whole new level.

When did you find yourself using the verses the most? Did one of the verses speak to you more than the others? If so, keep that one close—you can't overuse it!

So now that you know more about the Bible, has anything changed? Do you feel closer to God than before you started this journey? Miles closer? Incredible. Centimeters closer? Still incredible. Every bit, big or small, makes God happy. And all that great stuff is empowering and confidence building, which makes for a happier you.

Ten words can make a difference.

And guess what?

You can too.

ACKNOWLEDGMENTS

Ten Big Words was a labor of love in so many ways. I was able to do something I love — write. I shared ideas with people I love, and I got to learn so much about our God, the original giver of love!

Thank you to Amy Reger at Horizon Community Church, who asked me to co-pilot a fifth/sixth grade girls' Bible study, even though I kept telling her I didn't know what I was doing. Without her urging (or desperate need for warm bodies), *Ten Big Words* would have never happened. Thank you.

To my sweet husband, Jay, whom I held hostage on many a car ride, asking a zillion questions about the Bible, thank you. You are a wealth of knowledge and a patient, patient man. You are a great teacher, and you made my learning fun.

Friends and family who helped by listening, reading, encouraging and advising: Kristin Crowley, Becky Shoemaker, Tricia Spang, Jan and Ed Boldt, Karen Moran, Jennifer Michaelson, Maryellen Lengle, Sarah Youngblood, the McNeil girls and Jamie and Kristine Flerlage. Thank you for the wide variety of support you gave me. You are the best! God Bless.

xo,
Abby

WE WANT TO HEAR FROM YOU!

Go to:

www.tenbigwords.com

Instagram/Ten Big Words

Facebook/Ten Big Words

Let us know your favorite verse and when you turn to it. Do you have a ten-word verse you'd like to see in our next book? Please share it, and tell us your story!

Made in the USA
Lexington, KY
26 March 2015